Original title:
The Ocean's Soft Breath

Copyright © 2025 Creative Arts Management OÜ
All rights reserved.

Author: Adeline Fairfax
ISBN HARDBACK: 978-1-80587-419-5
ISBN PAPERBACK: 978-1-80587-889-6

Shelter of the Salty Breeze

In a hammock made of seashells,
Seagulls gossip, breaking spells.
Crabs in shades of beach ball hues,
Dance around with silly shoes.

Sandy toes and goofy grins,
Tidal waves do silly spins.
Mermaids juggling with some fish,
In this sun, we grant a wish.

Dreams Carried by Ocean Hues

Fish wear ties in iridescent flair,
Jellybeans float without a care.
Seashells play a game of tag,
While dolphins wear a painted rag.

The starfish burst into a cheer,
Announcing that the buffet's near.
Octopus throws a wild dance,
As crabs join in, they take a chance.

Secrets Held in Glassy Depths

Bubbles whisper silly tales,
Of lost socks and fishy scales.
A treasure chest with rubber ducks,
With candy wrappers, what a flux!

Giant squids with bowties bright,
Throw a dance party every night.
While sea turtles groove with flair,
They know life's good beneath the air.

Journey of the Wayward Wave

A wave with dreams to touch the sky,
Tumbles over, gives a sigh.
With foam that giggles on the shore,
It flops and rolls, and then there's more.

Wandering far, it trips and sways,
Splashing sailors in funny ways.
Crashes loud, then soft it curls,
To share its tales with ocean pearls.

Shadows in the Coral Gardens

Bubbles dance like clowns in suits,
They tickle fish with tiny boots.
Starfish giggle at a lost shoe,
While seaweed waves, 'Come join the queue.'

Crabs play poker, snipping shells,
While seahorses tell fishy tales.
A pufferfish joins in for fun,
But accidentally pops—oh what a run!

Caressing the Horizon's Edge

Seagulls squawk and steal my fries,
As dolphins leap with splashy highs.
They wink and joke as they swim by,
Making jokes about a flying pie.

The sunset laughs, a paintbrush bright,
As waves tickle surfers with delight.
Shadows chase as the tide comes in,
While crabs do cartwheels—where have you been?

The Enchantment of Seafoam Trails

Seafoam trails like frothy lace,
Whisper secrets in a cheeky place.
Clams recite their awkward rhymes,
While shrimps play chess with silly crimes.

A fish in a tux, oh what a sight,
Dances and twirls, oh what a night.
Starfish show off their best moves,
Leaving us laughing as the ocean grooves.

Lullabies from the Deep Abyss

Octopus croons in a calypso beat,
While mermaids tap dance on their feet.
A whale hums tunes with a goofy flair,
As sea turtles twirl without a care.

Eels snicker in their slippery suits,
Swapping jokes about floppy boots.
Underwater giggles fill the space,
In this ocean realm of goofy grace.

Caress of the Undulating Sea

The waves tickle toes like a silly dance,
As fish play leapfrog in a watery trance.
Seagulls swoop low with a squawk and a dive,
While crabs moonwalk as if they're alive.

Floating seaweed waves, like hats on heads,
Shout out loud with laughter, no one dreads.
A jellyfish jiggles, all funny and round,
Under the sun, where giggles abound.

Echoes in Shimmering Waters

Whispers of water in a playful tone,
Fish gossiping secrets like they're at home.
Starfish wearing sunglasses, looking so cool,
While turtles play chess, breaking all the rules.

The barnacles cheer, "We found a new game!"
As laughter erupts, they call out each name.
"Let's dance with the waves, no need to be shy!"
Even the clams are all saying, "Oh my!"

Secrets Beneath the Surf

With a flip and a splash, the sea critters play,
Whales tell tall tales that brighten the day.
Shrimps hold a party, disco lights they bring,
The octopus waltzes, oh what a thing!

Layers of sand hold treasures galore,
Buried old flip-flops, and maybe much more.
A sponge with a giggle says, "Not what you think!"
As pearls roll their eyes, they all start to wink.

A Symphony of Shells and Sand

Seashells chirping like they're in a band,
With starfish conducting, waving its hand.
The rhythmic lap, a thumping, a beat,
Even crabs are tap dancing — oh, what a feat!

The sea foam hums tunes, bubbly and bright,
As dolphins grab kazoos, it's pure delight.
A conch shell blows horns, it's a party on high,
As the waves cheer them on, under blue velvet sky.

Romance in the Briny Mist

Bubbles popping, fish in a dance,
Seagulls squawk as they take a chance.
Mermaids giggle, tails in a twist,
Who knew love could come from the mist?

A crab in a tux, what a sight to see,
He winks at a shrimp, 'Join a love spree!'
Even the oysters, they can't resist,
Falling for pearls, oh how they wished!

Light through Azure Ripples

Sunbeams dive, then they do the jig,
Splashing like toddlers, oh so big!
Fish wearing sunglasses, ready to glow,
While turtles in hats take it real slow.

A jellyfish floats, waltzing around,
Stinging like love, yet it's quite profound.
The seaweed shakes, caught in the fun,
Under the waves, it's a barnacle run!

Conversations with the Sea Glass

Sea glass chuckles, 'I've travelled afar,
Bouncing in waves, like a rockstar!
I've seen ships sink and crabs that sing,
And jellybeans drifting on a string.'

A bottle replies, 'Oh, what a plight!
I was a message, lost in the night.
But then I found kin in a driftwood ball,
Now we're a family, having a ball!'

Tranquility in the Nautical Night

Stars twinkle like fish that have caught a ride,
While dolphins leap, they toss their pride.
A starfish sighs, 'Just chill and soak,
Life's pretty funny; it's no joke!'

With surfboards made from dreams and foam,
The lobsters gather, feeling right at home.
They toast with shells to the moon's bright flight,
In the silly serenade of a nautical night.

Gentle Kisses from Distant Shores

Waves whisper secrets with a giggle,
They tickle my toes in a playful wiggle.
Seagulls cackle as they steal my fries,
While crabby critters throw me the eye.

Sandcastles crumble with a soft plop,
As I chase after shells—oh, what a flop!
Fishermen's tales swirl like fish in a net,
I laugh at their stories, can't place a bet!

Voyage of the Wandering Seafoam

Once a brave bubble, I sailed far and wide,
But tangled in seaweed, I couldn't abide.
With frothy companions, we floated away,
Making mischief in currents of play.

Riding the swells, I danced with delight,
Crashing on shore like an unwelcome sight.
"Catch me if you can!" I dared with a splash,
But the tide just giggled, then made a mad dash.

The Rhythm of the Lapping Tide

Here comes the tide with a splash and a lap,
It's a watery dance, or perhaps a mishap.
Frogs in the reeds croon a quirky tune,
While fish flip their tails beneath the blue moon.

Driftwood collects tales from long ago,
Like a lumberjack's tale, but oh so slow.
The stars wink down, tracking my plight,
As I twirl with the currents, what a silly sight!

Twilight on the Coral Tongues

The coral whispers with a cheeky grin,
As twilight unfurls, our evening begins.
Shells clank together like a band out of tune,
While crabs hold a meeting, beneath the pale moon.

Fish throw a party, complete with confetti,
"Dancing all night!" they cry, getting heady.
Sea cucumbers slide, in an odd little show,
Off the reef stage, they gracefully go.

Murmurs of the Deep Blue

In the depths where fishy friends roam,
Bubbles whisper secrets, like they're home.
A crab wears a hat, thinking he's chic,
While seahorses giggle, oh isn't it bleak?

In the reef, there's a party, a conch shell's the DJ,
Seaweed sways gently, what a wild ballet!
A dolphin does tricks, oh what a delight,
But watch out for that jellyfish, it's quite the fright!

Embrace of the Salt-Kissed Wave

A wave rolls in with a silly grin,
Saying, "Come get wet, throw your worries in!"
Starfish are lounging, in shades oh so bright,
While clams clack their shells, it's a clammy sight!

The gulls crack jokes, oh they're such hams,
While fish below swim in little clams.
A whale tells a tale, with a blubbering laugh,
It's a splashy affair, with a splashy craft!

Lullaby of the Starfish

Starfish lay snoring, all snug in the sand,
Telling the sea urchins, "Isn't life grand?"
A crab steals a snooze on a soft ocean bed,
Dreaming of treasures inside his shell shed.

Anemones dance to the tunes of the tide,
While sea cucumbers go for a wild ride.
A narwhal in pajamas, looks oh so sweet,
Whispers to dolphins, "What's for seaweed to eat?"

Dance of the Moonlit Currents

Under the moon, where ripples are bright,
The fish gather 'round for a dance in the night.
An octopus slips in a sequined dress,
Twisting and twirling, oh what a mess!

Crabs tap their claws to a clam shell beat,
While mermaids flip-flop, not missing a beat.
The night sky is watchful, the stars all aglow,
As waves tease the shore, putting on quite a show!

Tides of Tranquility

Waves dance like a clumsy fish,
Their splashes make the gulls all squish.
As jellyfish float with weird grace,
I giggle at their wobbly face.

Sandcastles crumble, much to my glee,
Tiny crabs plotting their escape spree.
Seagulls squawk in a comical flight,
As I run from the waves in sheer fright.

Starfish on shore seem quite aloof,
While kids chase foam like an undercover sleuth.
A flip flop's journey goes far and wide,
Perfectly complementing the ocean's stride.

Oh, how the beach tickles my toes,
While seaweed wiggles in funny rows.
Life at the shore is a giggling spree,
Where laughter and waves make a grand jubilee.

Embrace of the Ocean's Lament

Waters washing up with a sigh,
They tease the sand as if to pry.
A fish wearing sunglasses slips with flair,
While seahorses gossip and comb their hair.

Inky shadows swim beneath the sun,
As dolphins frolic, just for fun.
Sea turtles crawl like they're late for tea,
Grumpy hermit crabs scowl at me.

Beach balls bounce with zany spins,
While kids toss Frisbees aiming for wins.
Board shorts tangled like spaghetti in a pot,
Make beach days wild and never forgot.

But as the tide pulls with gentle yanks,
I'll share my snacks with grateful pranks.
For in this watery realm, you'll surely see,
That laughter and water are a perfect spree.

A Chorus of Salt and Silence

Seashells chatter, keeping it neat,
Like gossiping crabs with quick little feet.
They trade their secrets in a quiet tone,
As the tide hums softly, like a moan.

Surfers topple in a comical race,
While beach balls sail in a wild chase.
Flip flops flying with a delightful sound,
As children giggle and tumble around.

Mermaids laugh behind the coral trees,
While turtles munch on seaweed with ease.
The ocean's a party, a salty delight,
With waves that dance under the moonlight.

Yet, in the calm, a whisper can mend,
The chortles of fish who never pretend.
Their tiny jokes echo in the great expanse,
Inviting us all to join in the dance.

The Call of the Wandering Sea

Bubbles rise like jokes with a pop,
As fish swim by and do a flip flop.
The seaweed sways in a funky groove,
Making even the crabs start to move.

Seagulls swoop down for a snack or two,
While kids chase the waves in a bidding war hue.
Sand between toes equals pure delight,
As sunburned noses look quite a sight!

Dolphins giggle with a splashy cheer,
Their antics echo far and near.
With beach umbrellas dancing in a breeze,
Everyone's trying hard to find inner peace.

But wait, there's a splash, a mischievous spray,
I'll dodge the waves 'til the end of the day.
Life is a circus under the sea's decree,
Where laughter and water dance wild and free.

Soft Currents of Memory

A fish once wore a jaunty hat,
He swam right by a sleepy cat.
They shared a wink, then swam away,
Leaving bubbles at the end of the day.

The seagulls squawked, they danced on air,
While crabs in tuxedos had not a care.
One crab proclaimed, "It's time to feast!",
As he nibbled on a jellyfish beast.

A lighthouse blinked with comic cheer,
It whispered jokes for all to hear.
The waves laughed hard and rolled with glee,
While starfish giggled quite happily.

As shells exchanged some saucy tales,
The dolphins did their flip-flop trails.
But soon enough, they swam away,
Back to their jobs of playing all day.

Harmony in the Driftwood

An old piece of wood claimed to be wise,
It told of storms and shipwrecked lies.
But the barnacles laughed, "You're just a plank!",
"Where's your sea shanty? Or any rank?"

A dolphin chimed in with a splashy twist,
"I serenade fish; you're too old to resist!"
But the turtle, slow, just rolled her eyes,
"Why sing to fish? They're mostly disguised!"

Then came a wave with a frothy chortle,
"I play in the surf, I'm the real immortal!"
But the driftwood quipped, "You're just a scene,
At least I'm sturdy, I can't be mean!"

And laughter echoed in salty tones,
As creatures danced on the ocean's bones.
In driftwood's wisdom and laughter, they bound,
Together they danced, joyfully round.

Ripples of a Moonlit Dream

At midnight, crabs began to scheme,
To start a shellfish dance-off dream.
They twirled 'round rocks with all their might,
While minnows sparkled in the moonlight.

A clam said, "I've got the best moves!"
The others snorted, "Only if it grooves!"
They challenged her to break out in style,
But she just opened up with a grin and a smile.

Starfish winked with starry flair,
"Let's flip and flop like we just don't care!"
But octopuses tangled up in prayer,
"We can't all dance, let's just pretend we're air!"

Thus they twirled 'til the break of dawn,
With laughter ringing like a cool French horn.
They vowed to return, wild and free,
For every night was a dance for memory.

Caressing the Sorrowful Sailor

A sailor sat with his head in hands,
His ship transformed into a band.
The mast played tunes with the wind in stride,
While the waves clapped softly, a watery guide.

"Why so glum?" cried a pesky seal,
"Let's make some noise! It'll be a reel!"
But the sailor sighed, "I've lost my way,
These charts don't help when you're gone astray."

"Just close your eyes and hear the hum,
The sea sings sweeter; it's never glum!"
The sailor chuckled, joined in the song,
As fish did a wink, and the tides felt strong.

So from sorrow to laughter, his heart grew light,
The ocean whispered, "You'll be alright!"
With a song in his heart and a smile so grand,
He sailed on home, hand in fin, hand in sand.

The Breath of the Brine-soaked Air

Seagulls chat about their day,
While crabs breakdance in the bay.
A fish in shades of bright magenta,
Claims he's got the freshest agenda.

Waves whisper tales of sunken gold,
While seaweed wears its crown so bold.
A clam gives wink behind its shell,
Saying, "Life here is pretty swell!"

The tides keep trying to make a joke,
But seafoam laughs, and then it choked.
Barnacles join the marine ballet,
As dolphins flip with style today!

So, if you hear a splash or a cheer,
It's not a wave — it's just my beer!
The sand's my couch, the sun, my friend,
I'll stay here until the day's end.

Dreams Adrift on Salty Winds

A sailor dreams of fish that fly,
And tells his tales to clouds up high.
With sea foam beards and laugh so loud,
He claims he's king beneath the crowd.

Mermaids giggle 'neath the waves,
Calling sailors with their saves.
But each time he tries to make a catch,
He ends up tangled in a scratch!

The octopus paints with colors bright,
While jellyfish glow in the moonlight.
Bubbles float past with little glee,
"Hey, can we play? Count to three!"

So raise a glass to salty gales,
And let's sail on with silly tales.
For in this world beneath the sun,
Our laughter echoes, and we have fun!

Nautical Poems of the Hidden Depths

Down in the depths where fishies twirl,
A starfish tries to give a whirl.
He spins so fast, he lost a shoe,
Now he's stuck to a clam named Lou!

Crab's marching band makes quite the scene,
With sea cucumbers in their green.
They parade along the sandy floor,
But oops! One slipped and bumped the door.

Sharks in tuxedos swim with style,
They flash their smiles, and then beguile.
But watch your step; a stingray's there,
He'll tickle you, then disappear!

In the currents where the seaweed sways,
The fishy jokes will brighten days.
So join the fun, and take a dip,
In nautical cheer, we'll let it rip!

A Canvas of Aquatic Hues

Under the sea where colors merge,
Clowns fish dance and start to surge.
With every wiggle, they wear a grin,
While plankton twirls; it's a win-win!

Coral reefs boast polka dots,
While dolphins tease with clever plots.
They flip and splash, throwing spray around,
Until they land with a thumping sound.

A turtle named Ted thinks he's a star,
He rides the waves, claiming space far.
But when he trips and rolls in sand,
The fish all giggle at his bland stand!

With every splash, a cheer erupts,
In salty streets, joy corrupts.
So dive on in, enjoy the play,
In this aquatic world, we'll laugh all day!

Twilight's Glistening Embrace

As the sun dips low, a splash on my toes,
The seagulls are laughing, stealing my fries,
The waves tickle sandcastles, they're all in a war,
And beach balls are bouncing with mischievous sighs.

A crab in a tux, he's dancing around,
While jellyfish waltz without missing a beat,
The sunburned tourists are lost and confused,
Searching for shells, but they're finding their feet.

The tide pulls my flip-flops, they wander away,
I chase them with laughter, they giggle and roll,
The beach hat I'm wearing is claiming a life,
It flaps in the breeze like it's ready to stroll.

With twilight so glistening, silly and bright,
Funny fish leap high, in a splashy parade,
The stars start to twinkle, the moon waves hello,
While I dodge my own shadow that's ready to fade.

Undercurrents of Memory

In the depths of the sea, where the laughter hides,
A clam tells a joke, but it's lost on the waves,
Bubble-blowing dolphins swim by with a grin,
While octopuses juggle their hidden enclaves.

The starfish look serious, they're planning a heist,
As sand dollars giggle from under the shells,
The mermaids are gossiping, sharing a tear,
About fishermen's tales and their old castaway spells.

A fish in a bow tie, with sass in his fins,
He twirls and he dances, so full of delight,
The seaweed waves back, though it's lost in a wave,
In currents where memories float out of sight.

As tidal waves crash, from the depths they arise,
The laughter, it echoes through shells on the sand,
In playful positions, the sea comes alive,
Where secrets are buried and treasures are grand.

Serenity in the Gentle Surge

A gentle wave whispers, like a tickle machine,
It sways to the rhythm of flip-flops that dance,
Suddenly a seahorse rides past on a smile,
While crabs with sunglasses flaunt their romance.

The tide rolls and tumbles, then giggles away,
Shells laugh and sprinkle while kids splash around,
In puddles of joy, where their worries dissolve,
And sunburns become badges of fun on the ground.

A dolphin's acrobatics bring cheers from the crowd,
While the whales hold their sides, oh, what a circus!
The sun paints a canvas with laughter and flair,
And even the seaweed is dancing for us!

In the calm of the waves, with humor in tow,
Life's simple pleasures are surely the best,
The horizon calls gently with whispers of fun,
As we all play together, in nature's grand fest.

Horizon's Quiet Calling

The horizon is giggling, what a curious sight,
As surfers chase bubbles, they ride on the waves,
Where mermaids are sunbathing with wild, flowing hair,
And fish flaunt their scales in their sparkly knaves.

An old whale hums softly, a tune of the past,
While crabs form a band, with shells as their drums,
The tide rolls like laughter, it surges and swells,
Where each frothy wave whispers, 'Here comes the fun!'

A pelican squawks jokes, while diving for fish,
And the sandcastles fight like they're having a brawl,
The stars start to shimmer, the moon starts to grin,
As everyone joins in for the ocean's great call.

In the quiet of twilight, the fun doesn't stop,
With memories rising like bubbles in air,
We dive into laughter, embracing the night,
As the horizon keeps calling us all to the fair.

Beneath the Surge of Celestial Waves

A jellyfish danced, in a tutu so bright,
It twirled with the waves, what a comical sight!
Fish giggled and splashed all around in delight,
As crabs joined the conga under stars twinkling light.

An octopus wore glasses, reading a map,
He got lost in a whirlpool, what a funny trap!
Seahorses chuckled, and joined in the flap,
As he swam in circles, giving all a big clap.

A clam threw a party, with pearls as the prize,
The seaweed came dancing in glamorous guise.
But a rogue wave crashed in, much to the surprise,
Making all the guests dive, oh what a wild rise!

A dolphin popped up, wearing a bright hat,
Said, "Who ordered the fish tacos? This can't be that!"
And laughter erupted, as he did a splat,
In a splashy explosion, oh what of a chat!

Whimsy in the Ocean's Heart

A starfish with shoes strutted along the shore,
Said, "Walking in style? I can hardly ignore!"
Seagulls cawed loudly, "You're quite the encore!"
As waves rolled in giggling, asking for more.

A crab baked cookies, using sand for the dough,
They tasted of salt; oh, what a funny show!
Fish lined up to sample, their eyes all aglow,
But spat them out quickly, "This isn't the flow!"

A whale told jokes about fish in the sea,
Each punchline had bubbles, oh how they'd flee!
With every great laugh, they rose joyfully,
As a school of sardines danced, wild and free.

In a treasure chest hiding, a pirate did sleep,
Snoring so loudly, it made everyone leap!
But the gold was all gone, buried too deep,
And the fish rolled their eyes; it was just too cheap!

A Journey Through Briny Dreams

An otter in shades cruised on a big wave,
Sipping sea soda; oh, how he felt brave!
The mussels looked jealous, they wanted to rave,
But he tossed them some shells, "That's how I behave!"

A lizard sunbathed on a rock, looking cool,
But a wave splashed over, breaking the rule.
He shook off the water, "Ah, that's just my tool,
To create a grand splash—this is my school!"

A pufferfish puffed, trying to tell a tale,
But blew up so big, he scared off a snail!
They giggled together, sharing a laugh, without fail,
As they drifted in currents, on a whimsical trail.

A crab in a bowtie served lunch on a plate,
Where seaweed salad gave a twist of fate.
But a fish jumped up, "This isn't first-rate!"
While everyone joined in; they couldn't debate!

Chorus of the Gentle Swell

Waves tickle toes on sandy shores,
Seagulls squawk, oh what a roar!
The tide dances with a goofy glide,
As crabs do the cha-cha, side by side.

Mermaids giggle behind the coral,
In seashells, they hold a royal quarrel.
Fish in tuxedos swim with flair,
While starfish pose without a care.

Salty breezes tell silly tales,
Of rubber ducks and tiny sails.
Bubbles rise, then pop with glee,
The sun sets down for a cup of tea.

A treasure chest filled with lost socks,
Shrimps play poker near rocky docks.
Oh, what fun under the bright blue,
In this splash-tacular view!

Breaths of the Patient Seas

Fish in flip-flops swim around,
Doing the shuffle, what a sound!
A porpoise pranks with a coconut,
While octopus sings, 'Take a cut!'

The tides hum songs of fail and sway,
As jellyfish waltz in their own ballet.
Starfish crack jokes, but no one hears,
They're too busy laughing, shedding tears.

A crab wears glasses, reading a map,
'This route leads to a sailor's nap!'
Waves roll in with a giggly gig,
As the sun comes out with a bright, big wig.

Each splash a snort, each wave a rhyme,
Seagulls perform, trying to climb.
Underwater parties, what a delight,
Where even the seaweed joins the fight!

Whispers in the Calm After the Storm

After the ruckus, all is still,
Fish bust out their favorite thrill.
They're tossing shells, a game's begun,
Competing for laughs, not for fun.

Driftwood twirls like a dancing fool,
While seaweed sways, holding its rule.
Crabby judges, with claws raised high,
Reward the best with a salty pie.

Whales hummed tunes to lighten the mood,
While clams gave high fives, super crude.
The storm was tough, but laughter reigns,
In a watery world where fun remains.

Bubbles bounce, tickling the seas,
As everyone joins in on the tease.
A crabjoke lands, loud as can be,
Echoing across the blue with glee!

Laughter of the Anemones

Anemones chuckle in their fancy dress,
As clownfish join, bringing the zest.
They twist and twirl in a vibrant show,
Making waves giggle, from all below.

A sea turtle rolls with laughter grand,
In a barrel of kelp, taking a stand.
Jellyfish jiggle, doing a spin,
In the dance-off that draws everyone in.

With tickly tides and sparkly sprays,
Each day brings more funny displays.
A conch shell cheers, shouting, 'Bravo!',
As laughter rings out from reef to grove.

So join the fun, don't miss a peep,
With underwater stars who never sleep.
In the parade of joy where giggles flow,
The sea keeps secrets but shares the show!

Ballet of the Wind and Water

Waves twisting light as they dance,
A seagull wobbles, lost in a trance.
Shells giggle as they roll on the sand,
While crabs do the cha-cha, isn't that grand?

The fish in their bow ties all swish and sway,
Performing their moves in a graceful ballet.
Starfish applaud with their glittering hands,
While dolphins flip high, forming sea-breeze bands.

The breeze whispers secrets, tickling the waves,
Jellyfish juggle, oh, how it braves!
Each splash and each gleam has a story to tell,
As the sun dips below, bidding farewell.

As night cloaks the dance in stars' gentle light,
Big crabs take a bow, with all of their might.
So let's raise a toast to this watery show,
Where the wind pulls the strings, and we all just flow.

Breath of the Endless Blue

Bubbles are giggling, they sprint and they zoom,
Fish wear tiny goggles, but that's just their bloom.
Coral reefs laugh, what a rowdy shell game,
An octopus juggles, now isn't that lame?

The tide pulls a prank, as it tickles the land,
While crabs build a castle and wave with a hand.
Squids wear their smiles like balloons in the air,
As the seaweed dances, waving without care.

Oh, the waves have a wit sharper than a blade,
Rolling with laughter, a vast masquerade.
The sun, feeling clever, slips out for a swim,
While fish shout, "Hey buddy! The oceans look slim!"

And as nighttime draws close, with a wink and a gleam,
The tide pulls back gently, asleep in its dream.
Thus, life in the blue is a whimsical say,
A riot of jokes, in a watery ballet.

Whispers of the Tidal Light

The tide tickles toes with its playful embrace,
Whispers of waves hold a jellyfish race.
Sandcastles bobble under stormy delight,
As crabs in their hats say, "Now that feels right!"

Lobsters in sneakers jog up and down,
While flounders flip-flop, still wearing their crown.
The seaweed is gossiping, swaying with flair,
Spreading rumors of dolphins flying through air.

A clam with a shell phone is dialing a friend,
"To meet by the reef, it's a party to send!"
Barnacles bicker like kids at a fair,
As sunlight twinkles, they toss it with care.

And when moonlight casts spells from its silvery throne,
The fish disco dance with a glittery tone.
So, join in the laughter; let go of the fright,
For we all sway to whispers of tidal light.

Serenade of the Sardine Schools

Sardines in formation, a tight little crew,
Practicing tunes of the oceanic blue.
With fins all a-flop and scales all agleam,
They croon with a giggle—oh, what a theme!

Mackerels tap dance while anchovies sing,
Creating a symphony, oh, what a fling!
With bubbles for beats, they vibe with elation,
Performing for seals, an envious nation.

They wiggle and jive, spinning tales in the brine,
While krill form a chorus, oh, sweet divine!
Each twist of the tail draws a chuckle and cheer,
Grocery marketing might want to steer clear.

As waves pull their curtain in gloaming and shade,
Conga lines shuffle with shells in parade.
So let's toast to the fish and their musical schools,
For even the sea knows the joy of the fools.

Cradled by the Pelagic Embrace

I saw a fish with a tiny hat,
Dancing along like a wrinkly cat.
A crab tried to join but just lost his shoe,
And then bumbled out like a clumsy view.

The seaweed swayed in a funky groove,
While starfish cheered, trying to move.
With jellyfish jelly jamming around,
The party under waves was totally sound.

An octopus played on a saxophone,
As dolphins crowd-surfed, never alone.
They laughed at a whale who sang off-key,
A symphony of bubbles—so wild and free.

As tides tickle toes, they come out to play,
Among the barnacles, they frolic all day.
In the rhythm of waves, the fun never ends,
In a world where even fish make friends.

Reflections from a Turquoise Mirror

A seagull dropped a sandwich just by chance,
The fish below thought it was a dance.
They formed a line, took a tiny bite,
While shrimps in tuxedos sang with delight.

Sunbathers laughed at floating sea foam,
Waves piled high, it felt like home.
But when a wave splashed, it struck with glee,
Caught by surprise—'Who invited me?'

A crab in sunglasses strutted the shore,
With every step, he wanted more.
Seashells laughed; it's a sight to see,
A crustacean fashionista—oh, do agree!

As the sun set low, colors exploded,
Waves whispered secrets, and laughter eroded.
Each ripple a giggle, each splash a grin,
In this turquoise world, joy comes from within.

Emotions Carried by the Swell

As waves rolled in with a lively cheer,
A fish told jokes that we all could hear.
The tide joined in with a goofy laugh,
Creating a surf of a happy staff.

"Why did the crab never hug a seal?"
"A pinch too tight is just not a deal!"
They bobbed along, sharing quips galore,
A slippery roast like never before.

Pelicans perched with a keen sense of style,
While schools of fish swam, in single file.
A dolphin flipped with a grin so wide,
As a walrus belted out tunes, filled with pride.

With each splash and giggle, spirits did swell,
Chasing bright bubbles where laughter would dwell.
In this watery realm, the joy was profound,
Each wave whispered tales of fun all around.

The Sigh of Sandy Solitude

A single starfish found on the shore,
Sighs at the tide, 'Can I have some more?'
The crabs cracked jokes, all in good fun,
As gulls chimed in, 'Let's bask in the sun!'

The sand tickled toes, a fortress so grand,
As the sea rolled in, with a giggle planned.
Shells spoke softly, sharing tales so bright,
Of secret underwater parties, quite a sight.

One lonely flounder swam in circles tight,
He claimed he was just checking if all was right.
But the truth was out, he was lost in glee,
Just awaiting a floating party, you see!

As dusk painted skies with shades of delight,
Each wave whispered, "Wait for the next flight."
In the still of the night, stars shimmered bright,
Promising laughter and fun at first light.

Serenade of the Seafoam

The wave's a singer, full of cheer,
It splashes with joy, quite sincere.
A fishy chorus, off-key but loud,
They giggle in ripples, oh so proud.

The seagulls dance, with a funny flap,
As crabs join in, with a sideways tap.
Bubbles pop like silly jokes,
As sea turtles roll, oh what folks!

A beach ball bounces with a sploosh,
While starfish giggle, feeling the woosh.
The sun smiles down, for a heartwarming jest,
This watery party, we love the best!

So come, join in, don't miss the fun,
Where laughter and waves all blend as one.
With every splash, and chuckle combined,
The sea tells stories, one of a kind.

Murmurs from the Abyss

Deep down where it's dark, a whisper's heard,
A fishy giggle, quite absurd.
Octopuses juggle with shells in a line,
While sea urchins chuckle at the antics divine.

Nudibranchs prance in colors so bright,
They throw little parties every night.
Turtles play tag, what a comical sight,
And blowfish puff, then laugh at their plight.

Crabs throw a rave on the sandy floor,
Flashing their claws and begging for more.
In the depths, there's a quirky ballet,
The abyss isn't scary—it's just a cabaret!

So dive in deep, where the weird fish go,
With chuckles and giggles, it'll steal the show.
The surface looks calm, but oh, don't you fret,
The depths hold a circus you won't soon forget!

Secrets of the Endless Horizon

Under the sun, the horizon's line,
Winks at the clouds, feeling just fine.
With ships that tiptoe and try to be cool,
While dolphins are laughing—oh what a fool!

The sun throws a party, casting glints,
As mermaids gossip, sharing their hints.
The horizon proposes a game of charades,
And plankton performs as the spotlight fades.

The boats drift by with a cheeky wave,
While jellyfish glide, just trying to save.
From octopuses dressed as sailors in gold,
To seaweed that dances, oh so bold!

So capture the secrets this vista reveals,
With quirky capers and joy that appeals.
For at the edge of the world, in the light,
Are tales of hilarity waiting to ignite!

Cradle of the Coastline

On sandy shores, where giggles ring,
The crabs play hide-and-seek in the spring.
Seashells wear hats, quite jaunty and sweet,
While sandcastles melt—oh, what a defeat!

The gulls crack jokes with a salty twist,
As waves create tricks that simply insist.
A starfish winks, like a sly little guy,
While pelicans strut, oh, watch them fly!

Beach balls bounce with a cheerful thud,
And kites swoop down, a colorful flood.
The sun plays along, in a golden dress,
While sand between toes brings pure happiness.

So let's dive into this coastal delight,
With laughter and fun, it feels just right.
In the cradle of waves and the warm sun's glint,
Here in the joy, we find our own hint.

Caresses from a Shimmering Tide

A fish took a dive, said 'Oh what a ride!'
The wave gave a wink, that made it abide.
Seagulls laughed loudly, as they stole a chip,
While crabs did a dance, on a tiny tip.

The sun played peekaboo, with a hat made of foam,
Shells whispered secrets, 'We're never alone!'
Starfish had parties, with clams as the band,
Cartwheeling tiddlers, all painting the sand.

A dolphin did cartwheels, oh what a sight,
While a whale in the back hummed a tune of delight.
Crabs pulled their pranks, with pinchers so sly,
Even the octopus giggled by and by.

A starfish got dizzy, from too much sun,
But swam in circles, oh what fun!
They all held a toast, with bubbles and cheer,
'Here's to the sea, let's swim without fear!'

A Reverie in Foam and Spray

A shrimp wore a top hat, looking quite snazzy,
While jellyfish waltzed in a dance quite jazzy.
The tide brought a rhythm, a bubbly beat,
Where seaweed was swaying, all twisty and neat.

Conch shells chattered, passing gossip around,
As clams spread the news, up and down the ground.
'The tide tickles toes, come join in the fun!'
The anemones waved, 'Don't leave us undone!'

The water did chuckle, tickled by sand,
As fiddler crabs argued over their band.
They formed a parade, with sandcastles high,
While otters played fetch with a glorious sigh.

Urchins made patterns, like fashion statements,
Shells donned like jewelry held great entertainment.
A whale blew a bubble that floated so far,
It landed on seagulls, much to their bizarre!

Echoing Waves of Hope and Despair

A turtle once pondered, 'Where did my shoe go?'
While fish played tag, in a shimmering show.
The crabs sang ballads, in husky old tones,
Their shells clicked in time, like heartbeats of stones.

Seashells shared stories, of deep mysteries,
And coral forgot what it felt like to sneeze.
The starfish laughed loudly at sunken old ships,
'Guess they weren't ready for oceanic trips!'

A dolphin named Matt, lost his way in the whirl,
Decided to ask a wise clam for a pearl.
'Just follow the bubbles,' the clam did reply,
They'll guide you home fast, like a swift-footed spry!

But waves grew rowdy with giggles and glints,
As barnacles tapped, giving good-natured hints.
In the tide of confusion, they all found a cheer,
For laughter and splashes made everything clear.

Starlit Blush on the Sea Surface

At night, the fish sparkled like stars in a bowl,
With a whale crooning softly, 'I'm feeling quite whole.'
The moon chuckled softly, its light on the waves,
While crabs held a rap battle in sandy enclaves.

The otters made art with the driftwood they found,
'Let's build a big castle, a kingdom profound!'
Seagulls exchanged jesters, wore crowns made of pop,
With feathers and shells, they danced till they drop.

The tide played a tune on the shells of the shore,
As slippery flounders pushed hard to explore.
They all joined in chorus, a symphony sweet,
In the glow of the night, they twirled and pranced neat.

And there in the moonlight, they giggled and splashed,
With bubbles like laughter, their worries all dashed.
Stars blinked in approval, the night full of charm,
For funny, bright moments kept them all warm!

Remnants of Sailors' Dreams

Lost a shoe to the blue,
Thought it was a fish or two.
Sailing high on waves so spry,
Now I hear the seagulls cry.

I once caught a crab for fun,
Had a dance, oh, it could run!
It took my sandwich with a snap,
Now I wait for my next nap.

The compass spun, oh what a sight,
Pointing north, then left, then right!
A pirate's life, they said was grand,
But I'm lost with sand in hand.

So here's to dreams from a salty crew,
Mixed with laughter and a view.
As waves crash and seagulls glide,
We sing of journeys far and wide.

Tidal Serenade at Dusk

The tide rolls in with a gentle tease,
I lost my hat to a cheeky breeze.
Chasing waves in my trusty boat,
The seagulls squawking, I just float.

Waves croon a song, a funny tune,
I swear I saw a fish in a cartoon.
It winked at me, then slipped away,
Was it a dream, or just a play?

The sand tickles my toes as I groove,
A dance with crabs, they really move!
Jumping and jiving under the sun,
Silly moments, oh what fun!

As colors fade in the sky's embrace,
I laugh at the tide's silly chase.
Each wave a note in nature's song,
With every splash, I feel I belong.

Reflections in the Glassy Sea

A mirror of blue, so calm and bright,
I tried to dive in—what a fright!
Instead of fish, I met my face,
Splash! Oh dear, what a silly race!

The dolphins laugh as they glide by,
Winking at me with a cheeky eye.
They tease my float, it bounces high,
I grab it tight, oh me, oh my!

A seaweed crown upon my head,
I'm the ocean's queen, or so I said.
But then it slipped, oh what a scene,
Now I'm just a fishy queen!

With giggles echoing on the shore,
I'd trade my crown for laughs galore.
The glassy waves hold secrets deep,
Funny stories that make us leap.

A Meditation on Changing Tides

Oh, the tide pulls at my hopes and dreams,
Like a kid with candy, or so it seems.
It laughs as I chase, then slips away,
Leaving me wondering how to play.

The shells whisper tales of yore,
Of fish that danced on the ocean floor.
I try to mimic their flippy flair,
But just land awkwardly, all everywhere!

As sun dips low, everything's gold,
I stretch my arms, feel oh so bold.
But trip on a rock, fall with a splat,
The ocean chuckles, how 'bout that?

With every ebb and every flow,
I learn to laugh, let worries go.
For in this world of salty glee,
Laughter's the tide that carries me.

Ocean's Tender Touch

The waves go whoosh and splash,
Tickling toes as they crash,
Seagulls laugh, in frenzied flight,
Stealing fries with all their might.

A crab does a shuffle dance,
Claws up high, it takes a chance,
While sunscreen's smeared like war paint,
On a sunbather, looking quaint.

Flip-flops fly, it's quite a scene,
As sandcastles fall, so mean,
Kids giggle at their soggy fate,
With buckets, spades, and laughter great.

Mermaids take midday breaks,
Enjoying snacks and frosty flakes,
They gossip 'bout the human race,
Every splash, a comical chase.

Breath of the Sailor's Heart

Captain's hat on crooked head,
Sailing dreams, but no more bread,
Fish jump high like they're in flight,
Just to tease, then out of sight.

We spotted whales, or so we thought,
But it was just a floating pot,
Fretting fishes make a mess,
We'll never win this ocean chess!

Jellyfish in funky patterns,
Dancing lightly, like sweet spatterin's,
A shark shows up, but all it wants,
Is a snack; we're not its haunts!

The wind plays tricks on every sail,
Caught in a whirl, we laugh and wail,
A sailor's heart, with humor bright,
Is tossed and rolled in pure delight.

Whispers in the Briny Air

Salty whispers dance on skin,
As seaweed sings and lets us in,
Frogs in hats, they leap and croak,
At awful jokes, they laugh and choke.

The tide brings gifts like old flip-flops,
Tattered treasures from the shops,
A bottle floats, it says, 'Hello!'
But it's just sand, not much to show.

Waves roll in with a cheeky grin,
Pinching toes, letting laughter win,
A dolphin leaps with a silly sound,
As laughter echoes all around.

Seagulls gossip, with flapping wings,
About silly humans and their flings,
In the briny air, joy is near,
Nature's comedy, we all cheer.

Rippling along the Sandy Shore

Footprints scatter, chase the tide,
As crabs sidestep and try to hide,
A starfish screams, 'I lost my way!'
From rocks it rolls in sheer dismay.

Sandy shorts and sunburned noses,
Nature's gifts like prickly roses,
Everyone's busy, splashing around,
While laughter rises, joy abounds.

Kites soar high, like dreams untold,
A gust sends one into the cold,
And as it flops, the children shout,
'We'll save it yet, there's no doubt!'

Seashells huddle, keeping score,
Of silly antics on the shore,
With each ripple, a giggle found,
In sandy laughter, we are bound.

Murmurs of a Coastal Breeze

The seagulls squawk, a cheeky choir,
Chasing crumbs with keen desire.
A beach ball rolls with a willful glee,
While sandcastles fall, oh, woe is me!

A crab in a hurry, pinching my toe,
"Sorry!" he waves, in a frantic show.
The tide comes in, and my shorts get wet,
Oh, the friendships made, I won't forget!

Ice cream drips down, a sticky treat,
Seagulls plotting their daring feat.
With every splash, giggles abound,
A seaside smile is easily found!

As sunbeams dance upon the shore,
I trip on a flip-flop; oh, what a score!
The waves, they chuckle, good-naturedly,
In this salty realm of jubilee!

Heartbeat of the Tide Pools

Between the rocks, the creatures play,
Anemones bounce, oh what a fray!
Starfish lounge in a lazy mood,
While small fish dart—such a bold brood!

The seaweed sways, a greenish dance,
"I think I'll lurk," says the crab with a glance.
"Don't pinch too hard!" cries a clam in fright,
As waves crash down, oh what a sight!

A treasure hunt for shells galore,
Pockets bulging, who could ask for more?
The tide pools bubble with laughter and cheer,
Every splash is worth a wild cheer!

But watch out for snails moving too slow,
They wave and giggle, moving with flow.
In glimmering pools, the wonders thrive,
As the heart of the coast, we come alive!

Embracing the Horizon's Hum

A sunset painted with tangerine,
The clouds are fluffy, oh so serene.
Yet here's a gull, plotting a heist,
In hopes of snagging my dinner, so nice!

With every wave, a tickling tease,
I dodge the foam, feel the warm breeze.
Flip-flops fly as a kid makes a run,
Dashing for water, oh, what fun!

A kite flies high, dancing with flair,
While a dog chases, not a single care.
Laughter mingles with salt in the air,
At the end of the day, joy is everywhere!

As I settle down with toes in the sand,
I marvel at life, oh, isn't it grand?
Each moment swells like a gentle wave,
In this kooky world, we're all so brave!

The Language of Driftwood

A piece of driftwood claims it can speak,
"It once was a boat, but not sleek!"
The seashells giggle, they can't believe,
"Tell us your tales, please don't deceive!"

The barnacles nod, their wisdom profound,
"Once I was lost, but now I'm renowned."
They share their stories of wild, wild tides,
Of mysteries told where the sea secrets hide.

A rogue wave crashes, "I want the floor!"
Wood squeaks and cracks, "I've seen much more!"
Conversations swirl among frothy waves,
As the coastline listens, and happily raves.

In the sunset's glow, they laugh and thrive,
Each splinter whispering, "We're truly alive!"
Driftwood can chatter, with shells in accord,
In this world so buoyant, let's not get bored!

Echoes of the Water's Heart

A fish wore a hat, quite proud to swim,
He claimed he was suave, though his style was grim.
The crab laughed so hard, it danced and it danced,
While gulls hooted tunes, thinking they were entranced.

The starfish declared, 'I'm a five-pointed king!'
But all he could do was flail and fling.
The clams joined the choir, in shells full of glee,
Singing songs of the deep, quite out of key.

The seaweed swayed with a quirky twist,
Pretending to lead, shaking its green fist.
But bubbles popped up, saying it's not fair,
For the jellyfish waltzed, floating free in the air.

So if you hear laughter, don't turn with a frown,
It's just the sea's way of clowning around.
To join in the fun, come hop on a wave,
Where silliness swims, and lameness can rave.

Dance of the Rolling Swells

A dolphin in shades flipped with flair and sass,
He winked at the turtles that passed with some class.
They rolled on their backs, giggling like kids,
In a sea of pure joy, where the weirdness just bids.

The seagulls were gossiping about a big catch,
But all they had snagged was a slippery hatch.
A pirate fish grinned with a treasure map,
While swimming in circles, he took quite a nap.

The octopus spun, with eight arms in a whirl,
He painted the sea bed with colors that swirl.
And every time a wave brought the sun's bright glare,
They all waved it back with a splash of fresh air.

So if you see frolic beneath the blue sky,
Remember these moments, just let out a sigh.
For laughter is the tide's gentle coaxing glow,
In this sea-life dance, it's all about the show!

Veil of Mist Upon the Waves

The fog rolled in thick, like a sleepy old cat,
Wrapping up sea tales in a cozy old hat.
A whale took a snooze, dreaming of fish pie,
While the sea serpent yawned with a dreamy sigh.

The mermaids played poker, their shells were the chips,
With seahorses dealing, they'd throw some mad flips.
But who caught the cheater, well nobody knows,
For that tricky old squid was just going for bows.

A plankton parade skipped on bubbles so bright,
Enthusiastic and tiny, they danced into night.
And if you gave ear to the tales they would spin,
You'd laugh through the mists, while the waves let you in.

So next time you see a shroud of sea grey,
Watch closely for laughter that hides in the spray.
For beneath all the layers of mystery's thread,
Lies a riotous world where giggles are bred.

Tide's Embrace at Dusk

As the sunlight dipped low, the tide slid with ease,
Bringing sand pails filled with secrets and keys.
The hermit crabs donned their trophies with pride,
In a bizarre beauty pageant, they think they're bona fide.

The shore was a stage for a rock band of shells,
Each note a soft whisper, like ocean-bound bells.
Clams played the drums while the barnacles sang,
Giving rise to a bash where laughter just rang.

A surfer bird glided, a boogie on crest,
It tried to impress, but fell on its nest.
With a flurry of feathers and a comical splat,
Even the dolphins got into the chat.

So let's toast to the tide, with a splash and a grin,
For every weird moment we've had in the din.
With a wink to the dusk, as the sun bids adieu,
The sea hums a tune, just for me and for you.

Dreamscapes Beneath the Surface

Bubbles giggle, fish tell jokes,
Seahorses trot in silly cloaks.
Jellyfish dance in a jelly-like groove,
While crabs break out into a crabby move.

Seashells whisper, secrets they find,
A clam's big dream is to be quite blind.
Starfish play cards with the curious eel,
Each turn's a laugh, their fate surreal.

Octopus juggles rocks like a clown,
While turtles spin their shells upside down.
The deep blue is a comedy show,
With laughter that tickles the waves' ebb and flow.

In this realm where the absurd is king,
Mermaid choirs joyfully sing.
A waterslide made of seaweed curls,
Splashes of joy make the ocean swirl.

The Sea's Kind Lull

Waves embrace, a tickling quest,
Crabs in pajamas, they love to rest.
Anemones wave like they're in a dance,
While sea urchins joke, "Give us a chance!"

Seashells snore under blankets of sand,
A snoozing whale simply can't stand.
Dolphins dive deep for a nap in the blue,
While seaweed plays tag with its partner, too.

The sun plays peek-a-boo, bright and spry,
A playful pelican sails through the sky.
"Hey, look at me!" a fish shouts with glee,
"Catch me if you can!" to the jellyfish spree.

In these waters where silliness thrives,
Even the seaweed gets giggly vibes.
It's a lull that tickles, it's laughter that sings,
As the ocean cradles its whimsical things.

Breezes that Sing to Stars

Gentle winds hum a quirky tune,
Sea stars jiggle like they're on the moon.
A sand dollar dreams of being a dime,
While seagulls chortle, feeling sublime.

Clouds drift by with folksy flair,
Whales crack jokes, filling the air.
Tides pretend to be comedians slick,
With every splash, they slip and tick.

"Hey, sea cucumber, what's your best line?"
"Once I was a prince, but hardly a swine!"
Laughter echoes through twilight's embrace,
As the stars join in, dancing with grace.

In this realm where whimsy leads,
The breezes gather like playful seeds.
A symphony of chuckles beneath the sky,
As the night's gentle song begins to fly.

Sighs of the Forgotten Shore

Shells sit and ponder, their tales so grand,
Laughing at fishermen's empty hands.
"Remember that time we caused such a fuss?"
The tide just giggles, "Oh, what a plus!"

A crab waved goodbye to his silly hat,
Only to find it's a friendly mat.
Sand castles tease the waves with a dare,
"Come get us quick, if you really care!"

A starfish grumbles, "Why can't I twirl?"
While the breeze just dances, making it swirl.
Clams chuckle softly, hidden in the sand,
Imagining parties just oh-so-grand.

On the forgotten shore where laughter meets fate,
Even the barnacles join the debate.
As the night draws near, they sigh with glee,
For in these soft moments, they're truly free.

Creations from Shells and Driftwood

In the sand, a crab's got bling,
Shells and wood, it's all a fling.
Waves tickle toes, a gentle tease,
Driftwood's dancing in the breeze.

Seashell hats on sandy heads,
Fish on surfboards, talking threads.
Barnacles chat in a jolly tale,
While sea cucumbers set sail.

The sea gull's laugh, a squawk so loud,
Listening closely, you'll be proud.
Sea stars wear flip-flops, oh so chic,
Living their lives, not a single leak!

Crab races are thrilling, so much fun,
Shells collected, a shimmering run.
With driftwood crowns, they honor the sun,
In this wacky world, everyone has won!

Harmony in the Coastal Echoes

Salty tunes on a sunny day,
Seagulls squawk, come what may.
Shellfish rock band, surf 'n' roll,
With the tide, they lose control.

Walruses waddle, singing a beat,
Jellyfish jiggle to the salty treat.
Dolphins dive with brilliant flips,
While octopuses play airship clips.

Crabby dancers take the stage,
Tide pools spark their funny rage.
Lobsters tap dance, side to side,
Echoes of laughter, what a ride!

Clams in a chorus, a joyful roar,
With every wave, they want more.
Join the fun, it's a sandy scene,
Where everyone laughs, tangerine!

Dreamscapes of the Southern Sea

In dreamland's waves, the fish wear hats,
Surfing on bubbles, chatting with bats.
Mermaids giggle, twirling around,
Sharing jokes on their morning rounds.

Starfish practicing yoga poses,
Balancing on each other's noses.
Turtles trade tales of slow-motion,
Creating ripples of laughter's ocean.

Puffins play poker, cards in fins,
Laughing as they poke fun at sins.
An eel in shades, looking quite posh,
While squids throw confetti, oh what a squash!

Sandcastles grow taller with every joke,
While starfish bond, under the yoke.
In these dreamscapes, giggles roam free,
A silly sea of hilarity!

Celestial Sounds Beneath the Surface

Under the waves, a sound so bright,
Dolphins sing into the night.
A fishy orchestra plays a tune,
With bubbles dancing under the moon.

Crabs play maracas, with so much flair,
As clownfish trumpet, unaware.
Seahorses sway, in a rhythmic dance,
While starfish enjoy a bizarre romance.

Whales hum melodies, deep and low,
Tickling the seaweed, what a show!
Coral reefs echo the laughter in glee,
In this underwater jamboree.

Eels conduct symphonies, so refined,
With each gentle wave, laughter aligned.
Join the creatures beneath the brine,
Where bubbles giggle and all is fine!

Waltz Beneath the Moon's Gaze

Under the stars, a crab did dance,
With mismatched claws, it took a chance.
Seagulls laughed, they said, "Oh dear!"
While fishing nets snagged the cheer.

Turtles in top hats waddled round,
They tipped their hats without a sound.
A conch shell played a waltz so bright,
While fish performed with all their might.

The jellyfish glowed, a disco ball,
By seaweed, they'd twirl, and then they'd fall.
An octopus clutched a soda can,
Yet still insisted it had a plan!

As currents swirled around the scene,
The waves broke in laughter, crisp and clean.
With every splash, they shared a joke,
While dolphins bobbed, a joyful folk.

Whispers of Forgotten Shores

On the beach, sandcastles rise high,
Until a seagull swoops from the sky.
"Not today!" cried a kid with a frown,
As the tide rolled in to take the crown.

Crabs held meetings, secretive in style,
Debating if sushi was worth the while.
A clam was late, dressed in seaweed chic,
While fish giggled, their laughter unique.

The driftwood spoke of shipwrecked glee,
As starfish played cards, just you and me.
A crab overturned, it couldn't quite flip,
"Call for backup!" it cried, in a blip!

Shells made puns about life on the sand,
Waves rolled in, as if they had planned.
Together they laughed, a whimsical crew,
In the salty sea air, their worries flew.

Threads of Watercolor Horizons

Painting dreams on waves with a brush,
A fish swam by in a glittery rush.
"Are you an artist?" shouted a whale,
"Or just a fish trying to tell a tale?"

A squid wore glasses, trying to sketch,
With every line, the water would stretch.
Seashells critiqued with a glimmering grin,
"More blues and greens, and less of that fin!"

The sun dipped low, just like the tide,
Where dolphins leaped with a splashy glide.
A great pelican swooped down to peek,
"Is it just me, or is that fish a freak?"

With laughter echoing over the spray,
The ocean's canvas would sing and sway.
Every hue told a story untold,
As the waves giggled, bright and bold.

Serenity in the Sea Breeze

With a breeze that tickled the seagull's wing,
A starfish hummed an off-key swing.
"Bring me a drink!" it called with delight,
As tides curled softly, day turned to night.

Seashells rolled out a welcome mat,
While crabs played cards, all chilling flat.
A jellyfish floated, all lost in thought,
Whispering secrets the currents had caught.

The dolphins choreographed a show,
While plankton sparkled in a warm glow.
"More pirouettes!" they shouted with glee,
As the sea swayed in tranquility.

With laughter and joy upon every wave,
The sea breeze carried what none could save.
A concert of chaos, a playful zest,
In the heart of the ocean, we've surely been blessed.

Songs of the Cerulean Waters

In the waves where fish like to play,
Sea horses dance in a silly ballet.
Crabs wear hats, and the clams sing a tune,
While the dolphins juggle beneath the bright moon.

A whale's got a joke, but it's hard to hear,
He says, "Why splash? I'm already here!"
Seashells giggle, tickled by the foam,
As starfish argue about their sea-home.

Seagulls debate over fries from the shore,
Laughing at humans who beg for a score.
Turtles are racing all slow and steady,
While the sea cucumbers think they're quite ready.

So come take a dip in this watery show,
Where laughter floats in the tide's ebb and flow.
The sea's a comedian, with jokes galore,
And the tides always leave you wanting more!

The Dance of the Coastal Wind

A breeze tickles noses as it swings by,
Turning hats sideways, oh my, oh my!
The wind hums a tune that whirls through the air,
While sand castles tumble without a care.

A gull grabs a sandwich, oh what a feast!
The dance of the seagull is quite the beast!
While the kids laugh at puddles, making a splash,
The wind sets the party; it's all quite a bash.

Salty dog wags 'neath the bright sunny rays,
Chasing waves like it's all just a game that plays.
And the fishermen chuckle as lines tangle tight,
"Who's the real catch?!" they say, "What a sight!"

As the sun sets softly, the colors collide,
The wind still dances, no need to hide.
The ocean whispers jokes as dusk settles down,
A comedy show, no need for a crown!

Shimmering Tales from the Tides

Once a fish claimed he could jump to the sky,
But flopped in the air with a comical sigh.
The octopus chuckled while sipping a drink,
He exclaimed, "Don't worry, just learn how to blink!"

A sea turtle once donned a pair of fine shades,
Saying, "I'm cool, just look at my grades!"
The lobsters laughed 'til they lost all their claws,
In the midst of their giggles, a catfish lets pause.

The conch shell complained it was tired of blame,
It said, "Why's it always me? It's driving me lame!"
With tides all around and waves crashing loud,
The ocean's a stage that never feels proud.

So listen closely, you might hear the quips,
From whales who make puns as they dive through the flips.
The tales of the sea, wrapped in humor untold,
Keep us all laughing, both timid and bold!

Love Letters Wrapped in Seaweed

On a shore where sand and seaweed embrace,
Two hermit crabs write at a leisurely pace.
"I adore your shell; it's the best at the beach,"
"I cherish your wiggle; it's perfectly peach!"

A starfish declared, "You're my one and only,"
But the sea urchin just looked down, feeling lonely.
"Let's share conch shells and hide in the sand,
We'll send love letters, it's totally grand!"

The jellyfish glowed, lighting up the deep,
While barnacles hugged without making a peep.
Crabs sent their love notes stuck to a rock,
Hoping the tides wouldn't lead them to shock.

As the sunset painted the waves pink and blue,
Creatures confided what love means to the crew.
Wrapped in seaweed, their hearts float so free,
In this salty romance by the shore, can't you see?

Whispers of the Tidal Dance

The waves come in with a playful grin,
Tickling the sand like they're about to win.
Seagulls squawk in a comical flight,
Hey, is that lunch or a fishy fright?

Shells play peek-a-boo from their sandy beds,
Dancing with crabs on their tiny red heads.
Every splash seems to giggle and cheer,
As if the sea's ticklish, don't you hear?

Each tide rolls out with a silly sway,
Waving goodbye to the sun's bright ray.
And as moonbeams giggle and paint the sea,
It seems even Neptune loves a good spree!

Oh, how frolicsome the sea's gentle tease,
It pulls at our toes with mischievous ease.
With each lapping wave comes a chuckling sound,
In this watery world, pure joy can be found.

Gentle Waves Embrace the Shore

Waves sneak in like kids on the run,
Splashing their pals just trying to have fun.
Sandcastles crumble with a giggly poke,
Says the tide, 'Oh come on, it's just a joke!'

Seagulls swoop low, a playful dive,
Hoping to make the sand crabs contrive.
The beach ball bounces, no time to waste,
As surfboards glide with a flip and a haste.

Someone dropped a sandwich, oh what a sight!
Fish swim by wearing their best party light.
With every wave that rolls onto the land,
The spirit of fun fills the grainy sand.

So here's to the frolic, the surf, and the cheer,
The waves may whisper some secrets, oh dear!
The ocean giggles, with joy we implore,
Embracing the antics of this friendly shore.

Lullabies of the Deep Blue

In the deep blue, fish wiggle and wiggle,
Telling jokes that make even turtles giggle.
Their fins flap like hands in a joyful dance,
Sardines bounce by with a comical prance.

Octopuses juggle their shells with flair,
While dolphins jump high, tossing seaweed in air.
The seaweed sways, not entirely shy,
As if it too wants to reach for the sky!

Clams clap their shells, a rhythmic delight,
While a crab does the moonwalk, oh what a sight!
The deep blue sings, a merry, soft tune,
All under the watch of the bright, grinning moon.

Lulled by the giggles of creatures at play,
The ocean enchants at the end of the day.
With laughter and joy woven tight in each line,
The deep keeps its secrets but shares its good time.

Caress of Salted Breezes

A breeze arrives wearing a wild, blue hat,
Tugging at beach balls and chasing a cat.
With every gust comes a twinkling laugh,
As sand tickles toes, like a warm bubble bath.

The air's full of jest, a whimsical play,
It dances around in a breezy ballet.
Whispers of laughter float high and low,
As each salty wink puts on a show.

Kites soar above, wearing their brightest grin,
While children run circles, hoping to win.
The sun takes a bow, as shadows cavort,
In this salty playground, we all come to sort.

So, here's to the jerks of the wind and the sun,
Bringing joy in heaps and a lot of fun!
Each playful breeze brings a cheer to the day,
Making us chuckle in nature's own way.

www.ingramcontent.com/pod-product-compliance
Lightning Source LLC
Chambersburg PA
CBHW060112230426
43661CB00003B/159